Be Encouraged

Volume 1
2nd Edition

by
Olga Soto, MRC LSW LICDC

Copyright © 2023 by Olga Soto
All rights reserved. No part of this book may be reproduced or used in any manner without written permission, except for the use of quotations in a book review.

Be Encouraged Volume 1, 2nd Edition

ISBN 978-1-958818-02-2 Paperback
ISBN 978-1-958818-03-9 EPUB

Published by Take Heart Books LLC
Toledo, Ohio

take heart books

Cover Design by Olga Soto
Cover Layout by Take Heart Books LLC
Cover Art by Canva

Scripture quotations taken from
The Holy Bible, New International Version®, NIV®
Copyright © 1973, 1978, 1984, 2011 by Biblica, Inc ®
Used by permission. All rights reserved worldwide.

This work depicts actual events in the life of the author as truthfully as recollection permits.

This book is dedicated to the only person who deserves the credit,
the One who saved me from myself, and from death:
Jesus Christ, my Lord and Savior.

Purpose

What is my goal and what do I want to achieve through my writings? How do I want to use the gifts the Lord has given me?

Everything I do must point to Jesus Christ, my Lord and Savior.

I am blessed to have been given the gift to be able to express myself in words. I am so grateful that the Lord, the Holy Spirit, always interceded when I called on Him.

I have always had a difficult time being around people; the uncomfortableness came from the trauma I experienced throughout my life. But as I matured and grew to love the Lord, my desire to serve Him grew, as well.

Unfortunately, the trauma and anxiety that I experienced became a barrier and I found myself lost. But through my experiences and work in the field of social work–I found that I could love, be compassionate, and empathetic towards others.

The Lord blessed me with grace and mercy. He gave me the ability to reach out to others and teach others how to change their lives; teach others how to love themselves, and forgive themselves and yes, even come to look towards God as their source of strength. At times, I found myself praying and leading others to Christ who were open and needing a Savior.

So then, as I think about what is next for me, and I do hope to continue on in the social work field, I have considered what it is that the Lord has for me in the next season of my life.

I believe the Lord has answered that question.

I have been writing for a very long time. Recently, I began to hear God's Holy Spirit speak to me. He began to give me words which I began to write down. They are words of encouragement and direction; words of hope.

So, as I think about that question, What is the purpose of my writings? It is just exactly that–words of encouragement, words of direction, and words of hope for a better life filled with joy and peace. A life filled with mercy and grace as He has given to me.

God changed my life.

My transformation was not by the hands of a surgeon, although it was by "The Great Physician." Yes, God totally transformed my life and took away the desire for alcohol and drugs. He removed the desire to live in the world and sin. He taught me that there was a better life—a life without drugs and alcohol—a life of peace and joy.

I want to give back to others what the Lord gave to me: A REAL LIFE!

I am a sinner saved by grace.

I find myself repenting at least once a day (should be more). But my life is different now, my sins of today are not my sins of yesterday; although, I am still a sinner. No one is perfect, only He, who died on the cross for you and for me.

For God so loved the world that he gave his one and only Son, that whoever believes in him shall not perish but have eternal life.
John 3:16

The purpose of the essays is to guide, instruct and provide hope to those who read them.

- That the Lord be glorified through my writings.
- That the Lord would allow me to publish these essays so that,
- lives will be saved and transformed for His Kingdom, and then,
- those who are being transformed will continue the work as God reveals to THEM what THEIR gifts are, and
- how to use them for the saving of many lives for the Kingdom of God.

Then he said to his disciples, "The harvest is plentiful but the workers are few."
Matthew 9:37

Amen.

Table of Contents

Merry-Go-Round and Around 1
From Light to Darkness and Back 8
Consumed 14
People, Places and Things 20
Take That Step 26
Perspective 32
Saturated 40
Struggles 46
Stay in the Boat 54
The Well 62
Acknowledgments 69
About the Author 71

Merry-Go-Round and Around

Early on, while living with my grandma and grandpa, I was exposed to God.

Somewhere in the back of my mind I always felt like I had a connection to Him, ya know? There was even a time in my life (don't laugh) when I thought I wanted to be a nun. If you know me, you might find that humorous, but I believe that it was God's Spirit speaking to me; I just didn't know or understand it. I remember being at church and singing the songs as loud as I could, until my grandmother would get mad and yank on my little dress to make me sit. (Don't get any ideas—today, you won't find me in a dress.) She would give me that look, and I would laugh at her, well, with her. On our walk home, I'd sing the songs I had heard at church. I always felt that it was a connection to Him, but I wouldn't realize until many years later that He was there, always watching over me.

> "Are not five sparrows sold for two pennies? Yet not one of them is forgotten before God."
> Luke 12:6

Going nowhere: FAST

As a little girl, I was a happy kid and would love to play on the merry-go-round at the park. I always found it so fascinating that I could run in circles and never feel tired. Maybe for me it was a challenge to see how fast and long I could run and push the thing. It was comforting, giving me a sense of safety and protection. I didn't know it then, but I was developing a behavior pattern that would be difficult to change.

I was only about nine or ten when everything changed for me. One day I became like Forest Gump, and just started running and never looked back. Running and pushing became my way of coping; just running as fast as I could but never really knowing what I was running from or towards. That's kind of what life had been like for me as an older kid. It brings me pain to think about those days and running at a very young age. It wasn't that I wanted to run, it was just my way of coping with the chaos and conflict that existed in my little life at that time. Occasionally, I would have these moments of stillness where everything didn't seem so crazy and I was able to find rest, but then the chaos would start all over again and the screaming fears would have me jumping back on the merry-go-round.

Every now and then, I would sit in the middle of the merry-go-round and look up to the sky. I'd catch the rays of the sun and talk at God. *Are you there, God? Do you hear me, God?* That'd only last a minute. And then, oh no! Again came the chaos, the fear and pain.

Run! Push! Faster!
Where was God?
I need you. Do you hear?

I'm not nine or thirteen anymore, no, now I'm fifteen. That seems like an odd age to be on your own in a very large city. I've been walking all night and I'm tired. A sign says open at 11am, and it's only 7am. What do I do? Where do I go? There's nobody around to take care of me or love me. I've made everyone mad again. *Where is God?*

Years go by like this.

At such a young age I just did not understand that God

loved me because no one ever told me. "You are the problem, you go run, run, run and stay out of the way," is what was said to me. I thought I was hated by everyone. I had caused a lot of problems and I thought everything that was wrong was my fault. Back to the merry-go-round, the only safe place that gave me a sense of peace, even though I was alone.

There were moments when I thought, *Ok, it's ok, you can stop running*. But then the madness would start all over. Another black eye, a punch, a kick—a slap. Run to the merry-go-round! Run and push! All I wanted was a normal life like other kids, like back when I was seven and eight. *Where is the laughter? Where is the singing? Will I ever sing again?* There were moments when I would get so tired of pushing and running, but I felt that if I stopped, the consequences would be too much. I didn't know there was any other way. What I knew was that as long as I ran from place to place and as fast as I could— I would be safe. I didn't know then that it is Jesus that loves and saves. I was running on adrenaline and fear and that's how I kept going. I was going so fast that I couldn't see anything but fear, like tunnel vision. It pushed me to run to the only place I felt safe. I jumped back on the merry-go-round.

It's About Trust

I'm getting tired. It's been years now and I mean years of PTSD: anxiety, fear and depression.

God, where are you? Can you hear or see me, God? Ok God, I really want to get off of this merry-go-round.

You know, sometimes times when I would stop here and there, I can remember hearing, "Jesus loves you, come to Him, come just as you are." *What do you mean God wants to love me? What do you mean Jesus loves me?* I had been told over and over by many people, "You're not good enough for anyone to love you," so I didn't think I was.

I thought that God was only for GOOD people.

What do you mean we have all fallen short of the glory of God?
What do you mean he was wounded for me?
Why would he let Himself get hurt for me?

I didn't understand. I wanted to understand. I thought that God only loved special people and I didn't feel special.

Are you sure? I'm special? You're special? Everybody who wants can be loved by God? OK, tell me more about this wounded stuff, He died for me, and He wants to heal me... Heal me from what? I'm so confused. You want me to stop and trust God, you say?

But I was afraid to let go, to take my hands off the merry-go-round and put my hands in His.

Oh Boy, you want me to listen to this scripture.

> But he was pierced for our transgressions, he was crushed for our iniquities; the punishment that brought us peace was on him, and by his wounds we are healed.
> Isaiah 53:5

What are you saying, Jesus loves me that much that he would allow someone to hurt him, for me... why? I don't understand why he would die for me. What, so I could be healed? Are you kidding me? You mean I can stop running? I don't have to run anymore? I'm tired. My legs are tired of pushing the merry-go-round of my life and going nowhere.

I was confused and tired and I didn't know it then, but I began to pray.

> *Oh Lord, thank you that you gave your life for me that I could live. You waited for me for twenty years. I must be honest with you, Lord, all of this running doesn't seem to stop, I even run in-*

side of myself. I can be sitting in chair and I feel my body want to run. I have no stop button or at least I can't seem to find it. Help me, Lord, slow me down and help me, Lord, not to be afraid— but to trust you. I know you want me to let go of the merry-go-round and trust you. You want to carry me. Help me, Lord to trust you because I have no trust left for anyone. Jesus, I love you, help me to trust you. I'm just being honest, Lord, and I think you appreciate my honesty. For the first time I am being honest. Here I am, Lord, thank you, God. I'm slowing down and I can feel the merry go round… slowing down. I feel… my breathing… slowing… a few minutes ago my heart was coming out of my chest, but as I learn to focus… on You… Everything… begins to slow, slowing down… I'm letting go… of the merry-go-round. But forgive me, Lord, I might need it every now and then until I can completely let go… I know You will stand by me and give me the strength to stop and surrender to You. Ok, Lord, what else do I have to do to surrender my fears and my life to You? What steps do I need to take to know You more? God help me, I want to run.

And He said:

> Trust in the Lord with all your heart and
> lean not on your own understanding.
> Proverbs 3:5

Step 1: Trust Jesus NOW.
Just trust Him.

> If you declare with your mouth, "Jesus is Lord,"
> and believe in your heart that God raised
> him from the dead, you will be saved."
> Romans 10:9

Step 2: Admit that I am a sinner and that I need God's help.
Are you kidding me? What have I been saying? Ok, I'm a knucklehead and it took me a few years —only about twenty.

> My son, give me your heart and let
> your eyes delight in my ways.
> Proverbs 23:26

Step 3: Be willing to turn your life over to Him completely.

Wait a minute. Everything? All of me? But God, I like some of me. What, You'll remove the mold off of the cheese and we will still have some good cheese left? Cool. Let's do this. I'm getting excited to see what you're going to do, Lord.

Step 4: Believe that Jesus Christ died, was buried and rose from the dead for me.

Are you kidding me? What have we been talking about? Didn't you read the verses above? "He was wounded for my transgression and by His wounds I am healed."

Step 5: Invite Jesus into your heart.

Give your life to Jesus and tell Him you want Him to be your personal Lord and Savior.

Give Him control. You can take your hands off now, just give Him control. SURRENDER.

> 6 Humble yourselves, therefore, under God's mighty
> hand, that he may lift you up in due time. 7 Cast all
> your anxiety on him because he cares for you.
> 1 Peter 5:6-7

Step 6: Pray all of the above and ask the Lord to show you how to get off of your merry go round.

Jesus wants to save you today. This very minute. Don't wait. Give your life to Him. He knows how tired you are.

He is waiting for you.
Amen.

From Light to Darkness and Back

*You know, this is going to get a little deep.
If it's too much for some of you to read, then I suggest
you don't. BUT maybe you're a little curious about
what I have to say?*

I have always had this recurring image: there's this little girl sitting in a driveway, playing with rocks and singing at the top of her lungs. She's trying to drown out the thoughts in her head—she doesn't want to hear anything coming from within or out.

I learned at an early age how to silence my own thoughts. I learned how to space out quickly. I used to think I would never see light or joy again and that there would always be a cloud of darkness hovering over me. What I did not understand then, was that this darkness was called Depression.

From my beginning I would have a recurring image that I was swimming in a pool of alcohol. Yes, I said alcohol. No, not a pretty sight, but, yes, that was my image. I would sit and stare out into space and I'd see myself as a baby swimming in what looked like alcohol. It had the same color; I could almost smell and taste it. I used to believe that's why I became an alcoholic—because I was born in it.

Little did I know the Lord would use that image to show me how He had always been with me from the that very beginning. The Lord would reveal the truth of these recurring images.

That little girl sitting in the rocks, singing her heart out and the baby swimming in alcohol—those weren't the first images I had.

Let me tell you about the *very* first images I ever had:

There's a little girl sitting on the front stoop of her grandmother's home. She has her favorite saltine crackers. She is singing and laughing and happy with not a care in the world. But then the image transforms into darkness. There is a black cloud hanging over her. She's singing loudly but she can't sing loud enough. She is trying not to listen to the distant noise—what is coming toward her—but she can't drown it out. She thinks if she sings louder, then maybe she will keep the warm sunshine on her face and maybe she will keep the happiness and joy. Maybe.

> You, Lord, keep my lamp burning; my
> God turns my darkness into light.
> Psalm 18:28

It wasn't until years later when I gave my life to the Lord that I began to know and understand the power of God. His magnificence, grace and mercy bestowed upon us sinners are a blessing that I never deserved. God used images to speak to me. This is how the Lord has spoken to me all my life and whether you believe me is not for me to convince you.

When I look back in time, I can see the same little girl playing in the front yard but now she is twelve and she hears: you will be a social worker. Years later, when I became a social worker, the Lord brought back that memory of the twelve-year-old girl and His words to her.

Through each phase of my life—good or bad, God's hand has been there every step of the way. He wants to be there for you, as well. God is waiting for you to take His hand. Let Him lead you. Give Him permission to come into your life and guide you.

> Trust in the Lord with all your heart and lean not
> on your own understanding,in all your ways submit to him, and he will make your paths straight.
> Proverbs 3:5-6

So, let's look at that first image. What does that mean? Well, I think that the Lord brings to our remembrance the people in our lives who brought us joy and happiness. I think that image has remained ingrained in my mind all these years so that I could know what the Lord was going to give back to me. Those were the joyous times for me—when I was a little girl who was loved and cared for. I thank the Lord for preserving those memories and showing me that I am still His delight, just like I was to my grandparents. God is showing me that I am adopted into His family and He wants to tell me that He has not forgotten about that little girl. He wants to show me that the same daddy that loved that little girl is the same daddy that loves me now.

Praise God! What does He say?

He says, "I will never leave you nor forsake you."

Years later, I realized that all I had to do was humble myself before Him and then all of the darkness that hovered over me would just disappear because He wanted to replace it with joy, happiness and victory.

> For the Lord takes delight in his people;
> he crowns the humble with victory.
> Psalm 149:4

Amen.

So, let's take a look at the second image. All of my life I have carried this image. I used to believe I was drowning in alcohol. I really used to believe that. All I could see was this yellowish liquid and I was literally swimming in it. I would close my eyes and there it was: a child swimming in this ugly, yellowish water. It's not a pretty one, right?

That's what I thought, until recently when I was sharing this image with a person whom the Lord used to show me otherwise. I praise the Lord how He used this person to help me see the truth of that image and not the lies that Satan wanted me to believe. This person prayed with me and asked the Lord to reveal the truth of that image. I couldn't believe that all these years Satan had convinced me that I was drowning in alcohol, that I would not be worth anything, and that alcoholism was meant to be for me from the beginning of my life.

It was a WOW moment!

Friends, the truth of that image—oh, my goodness! The moment the Lord revealed to me the truth of that image I was set free from the lies and manipulation of the enemy!

Here is the TRUTH:

> His splendor was like the sunrise; rays flashed from his hand, where his power was hidden.
> Habakkuk 3:4

Check it out—that yellowish substance that I thought was alcohol…? It was not alcohol AT ALL.

From my vantage point, and from what Satan wanted me to believe, it very much looked like it. But I know now that it was God's hand over me. It was His radiance and His light covering me. He was there, the whole time, protecting me and covering me with His Spirit, keeping me safe.

Praise God!

Amen.

> "Before I formed you in the womb, I knew you, before you were born, I set you apart; I appointed you as a prophet to the nations."
> Jeremiah 1:5

Now I'm no prophet, I'm just a child of the King who was chosen from the very beginning of time. The Lord had His eye on the sparrow, He has watched over me from even before I was born.

GOD DOES NOT LIE.

If you feel there is no purpose for your life or if you feel like you are not important, then I am here to tell you that is a lie from the pit of hell.

God is NOT a liar, and you are the most important thing to Him. He wants to give you life and purpose.

I leave you with this:

> But you are a chosen people, a royal priesthood, a holy nation, God's special possession, that you may declare the praises of him who called you out of darkness into his wonderful light.
> 1 Peter 2:9

> "For I know the plans I have for you," declares the Lord, "plans to prosper you and not to harm you, plans to give you hope and a future."
> Jeremiah 29:11

Amen.

Consumed

What does that word CONSUME mean?

Merriam-Webster defines *consume* as a transitive verb…

Huh? Furthermore, *consumed* is to waste or burn away; to PERISH.

Wow.

That sounds exactly like my life before Christ.

I was wasting away, and my life was headed towards death. When I think of that word *perish*, I think of a physical death. Dead. Buried in the ground. The life that I was living—consumed by the world of drugs and alcohol, consumed by the selfishness of what I thought the world could offer me—was sinful.

What does it mean to be consumed by one thing that takes up your whole life, mind and soul?

Well, in my case, I was consumed by the lies of the world and the desire to be loved and feel needed. I was so consumed that I put myself in situations and I did things that, if not for the Lord, I would have been dead. I should have perished at the hands of the world.

Our feelings of emptiness, and the need to be loved and give love, consumes us to the core and to the depths of our existence. The fear of dying alone can consume us to the point of compromising any and all moral values. We sabotage the good in us. We compromise for the sake of that single moment to fill the cup of our emptiness.

We become consumed to the point of saying:
I will risk one more day, one more moment,
no matter the consequences.

We forget that we are an extension of what God has placed in our hands and those we are responsible for—our children, our loved ones, our very own lives. You know back in the day the word consumption was also used to describe Tuberculosis, which is defined as "a progressive wasting away of the body."

God's word describes sin in this scripture.

> All of us have become like one who is unclean, and all our righteous acts are like filthy rags; we all shrivel up like a leaf, and like the wind our sins sweep us away.
> Isaiah 64:6

We go through life day after day, week after week, month after month and yes, year after year, being slowly, but progressively, swallowed up by the darkness of the world. We wait and we ask who or what will rescue me from this abyss? I gradually found my life in this hole only when I looked up from the abyss and cried out: WHO WILL SAVE ME FROM THIS DEATH?

I remember so clearly God speaking to me, even in my unsaved life, as I sat in a dark apartment crying out to Him, "Save me, God! Save me, Jesus! I don't know who you are, but I've been told you love and want me to have a better life! I have been told that you will forgive me for consuming and giving my heart, soul and mind to this world!"

As I lay there on the floor, my eyes closed, I felt surrounded by a pool of water, drowning in my sins. My body was sinking deeper into the abyss, but I looked up and I saw a light. I stretched my hands through the water and the Lord grabbed me and saved me that very day. God pulled me out of the depths of my sin, and He said to me, "I want to save you."

Thirty-six years ago, in that dingy apartment the Lord rescued me from sin and death.

Is God speaking to you?

Have you become consumed by the world or have you become consumed by something that has become a distraction and taken you away from hearing God's voice?

What I learned from that moment is that I will physically wither away—that is true for us all. But what I needed most was to RECOGNIZE that I was walking around spiritually dead, and I was so consumed by the world that I had neglected my relationship with God and with the Lord Jesus. I had no relationship with Him. The only relationship I had was with the world and that was destroying me.

Have you found yourself consumed by the need to be loved and feel needed? I am here to tell you that the Lord loves you and wants to provide for all of your needs. He wants to give you a life that you have always wanted! He wants to give you a life of happiness, peace and joy. God calls us to surrender our lives to Him and to consume ourselves with Him. You might be experiencing some fear of turning your lives over to Him. The fear of the unknown. I totally get it; I had that fear, too. The fear of not understanding what I was getting myself into and what does it mean to surrender my life to Him… Well, here are some steps that I think you'll find helpful. Come on! I will be right here with you and so will the Lord. Think of it this way: you have given your life to the world and it has brought you nothing but sadness, depression, loneliness and fear.

Let's start with looking at scripture. Get a bible. If you don't have one in your home, you can download a bible app on your phone. Or, if you are not able to do that you can read the verses here. Whatever your situation, the Lord provides you a way to receive His word.

Begin by praying: *Lord, I am ready to surrender my life to you. I am afraid, Lord. I don't know what to expect but I believe my life needs to change and I am ready for You to change it. Help me, Lord, not to be afraid. Help me, Lord, to trust You. Give me the strength and courage to let go of my fears. Help me, God, to open my mouth and confess that I have sinned against You. Forgive me. Thank you, Lord, that you accept me with open arms. Here I am, Lord, take my life and make it what You would have me to be. In Jesus name I pray.*

Amen.

Let's read some scripture.

> Trust in the Lord with all your heart and
> lean not on your own understanding.
> Proverbs 3:5

Now is the time for you to really trust the Lord. You have been trusting everyone else, but God is saying, "Trust me. I will not fail you. Let me give you a new life. Just follow me."

> Give thanks to the Lord, for He is good!
> His love endures forever.
> Psalms 136:1

Wow!

God has loved you all of your life and He has been right there waiting to love you and restore your life!

And just what has He done for you?

JESUS DIED ON THE CROSS FOR YOU AND FOR ME.

He died so that we could be saved from this consuming world that has robbed us of joy, peace and most importantly the love of Jesus Christ—the Giver of life.

You think you have seen love? You have experienced "love" that was hurtful and dangerous to your life. Jesus loves you as His best friend. He wants to restore your life. Would your best friend die for you? I doubt it very seriously. I don't have a single friend that would die for me and surely not one from my past. If anything, my "friends" left me. They abandoned me. They lied to me. They cheated on me and beat me; left me for dead. But my God! Now, my Jesus, He is my best friend! Hear what His word says.

This is what He did for me and you.

> Greater love has no one than this: to lay
> down one's life for one's friends. You are
> my friends if you do what I command.
> John 15:13-14

And also:

> Love the Lord your God with all your heart
> and with all your soul and with all your
> mind and with all your strength.
> Mark 12:30

Ok, if you have taken these steps and are still afraid, then just stay close to the Lord. Consume yourself with His word by getting involved with a bible believing church and joining a bible study where you will get fed with the word of God. Make a choice to leave the world.

Begin a walk with the Lord and cling to this decision.

> "Be strong and courageous. Do not be afraid or
> terrified because of them, for the Lord your God goes
> with you; he will never leave you nor forsake you."
> Deuteronomy 31:6

Amen.

People, Places and Things

Things, things.
What are they? What do they mean?

We put so much emphasis on things. Things that keep us from the Lord. Things that bring us down; things that trip us up. Things that cause us to act foolish and bring us pain, anger and heartache. I never had many things; I always wanted things. Just like the next person, I wanted things that I thought would bring me happiness, peace and fill my emptiness.

It's like I was far off in the distance and I could see all of these things lined up one by one, and I would go to pick them up. Each thing had a name. A name of a thing or a person and I was deceived by the allure of the thing— like how pretty it looked or how handsome he was. The joy and happiness I would feel when I looked at that person… all lies! These things all seemed to be filling the emptiness of my heart that only wanted love.

As I stood and pondered on these things, I was taken in by what I heard, "I will bring you joy. I will make you happy. I will take care of you and you will always be happy. All you have to do is trust me. Believe in me. Give me your mind, soul and body. Look at all these things I can give you. Look at the places I will take you! Take my hand and trust me."

We, as humans, are not the only ones that are tempted by the allure of people, places and things.

> Again, the devil took him up to a very high mountain and showed Him all the kingdoms of the world and their splendor. 9 "All this I will give you," he said, "if you will bow down and worship me."
> Matthew 4:8-9

I am ashamed to say that I fell for the temptations. I believed the devil when he offered me happiness, joy and success.

I can't tell you the number of times I fell for his lies. I was manipulated by the loneliness and the emptiness in my heart. I was manipulated by (are you ready for this?) the choices that I had made which got me into trouble to begin with.

It was a vicious cycle.

My emptiness and loneliness led me to make poor choices in the people that I associated with, in the places I went, and in the things I chose, which ultimately led to my fall, and then my salvation. I fell for the lies. Satan showed me all of these beautiful things and he deceived me, and I believed him. I was blinded by my sinfulness, and because I did not know the Lord to show me the right way—I took the wrong one.

> Be alert and of sober mind. Your enemy the devil prowls around like a roaring lion looking for someone to devour.
> 1 Peter 5:8

And oh boy, did I get sucked in by the lies and manipulation!

PEOPLE that lied to me and their words that I can hear over and over, "I want to love you like no one else. I want to take care of you like no one else. Trust me. Believe in me."

THINGS that looked pretty. We are so vulnerable to the schemes of the devil and he is out there prowling around waiting for someone to devour. In our weaknesses we neglect to listen to others, or to God, and all of our emotions have surrendered to this person, to whatever **PLACE** they want to take us and to the things we think we need.

And just what is the goal of the enemy?

The goal is to destroy us. To keep us from the one person that can save us, change us and give us a better life. The one who can give us direction so that we do not continue to make the same mistakes over and over again. That person is Jesus Christ, and the enemy is at war with Him for our very soul.

> The thief comes only to steal and kill and destroy; I have come that they may have life and have it to the full.
> John 10:10

It is easy to judge those that have been taken in by the enemy's schemes. Those that have almost destroyed their own lives by the choices and decisions they have made—the people they have brought into their lives and the places they have gone.

But the Lord reminds me continuously in Romans:

> For all have sinned and fall short of the glory of God.
> Romans 3:23

Praise God He has made a way out for us! Praise God. Thank you, Jesus, for dying on the cross for us! Thank you, Lord for making a way out for me and others. Help me, Lord, to remember that those also means us, as we all have "sinned and come short of the glory of God."

People, places and things.

I learned to trust the Lord and He replaced all of the hurtful people in my life with Godly people who love and accept me for me. God wants to weed out those people that have no place in your life. He wants to be first place in your life so that you can receive blessings instead of curses. God wants to bless you with things that you need and things that will bring you joy.

God IS NOT opposed to happiness and joy!

God IS opposed to rejecting Him for people, places and things. God wants us to be prosperous! He wants to bless us, and He gives us a choice.

Early on in my walk one of the first scriptures that the Lord gave me, which I have carried close as a reminder of the promise God made to me, was based on two options. He was asking me to make a choice that would bring one or the other—blessings or curses. God's Spirit spoke to me that day some twenty years ago and I knew the right choice would make a huge impact not only on me, but it would break "the generational curse" the enemy had on me, my children and even their children. I understood the huge impact my decision would have because after umpteen years of living my life for people, places and things, I was finally ready to surrender. The white flag was waving because I was tired.

I had enough.

The fear that overtook me that day, the fear that my children would continue in the same path I had taken was too much for me to bear. There had to be another way. There had to be a better life and I knew I could not give that to them without making a drastic change first in my own. I needed someone else to take charge of my life because I had made a complete mess of it. It was time to stop being selfish and only thinking of myself. God knew this was the time and He "made me an offer I could not refuse."

Just listen to this offer, listen to the choices God gave me and He never forced me to make the right one. He already knew I would because He knew I would choose Him and love Him.

It was a WOW MOMENT.

> This day I call the heavens and the earth as witnesses against you that I have set before you life and death, blessings and curses. Now choose life, so that you and your children may live 20 and that you may love the Lord your God, listen to his voice, and hold fast to him. For the Lord is your life, and he will give you many years in the land he swore to give to your fathers, Abraham, Isaac and Jacob.
> Deuteronomy 30:19-20

Which are YOU going to choose?

Take That Step

Life can be difficult. Fears overcome us and keep us from taking the steps the Lord calls us to take.

God understands our fears. He does not like our fears, but He understands them. God calls us to trust Him. Take His hand and allow Him to guide you, guide your life in the direction of freedom. Freedom from what, you say? *Freedom to what? I don't understand, God. What are You calling me to do? What is it I'm supposed to do, God?* Well, unless you listen to Him, unless you are obedient to Him— you will never know what He has in store for you.

Is God calling you? Is He making your heart beat out of your chest? Can you feel Him pulling at you? Can you feel Him calling you? What is it that you are sensing? Is it like something you have never felt or thought? Are you awakened in the middle of the night and can't understand why you are restless?

I remember that feeling.

I remember that sense of urgency to get back to sleep and I couldn't. In the beginning, I couldn't understand what it was or how to get rid of that feeling. I had to learn that God was waking me up because He wanted to get my attention.

God was telling me, "There is sin in your life that you need to get rid of."

And I would ask, "What sin, God, do You want me to get rid of?"

"All of your sin."

I was confused. What is it that I need to do and what is the first step I need to take to free myself from the darkness that I feel?

What Lord, do I need to do? Tell me, Father. Please speak to me God. What step do I need to take? Help me Lord to understand because I am tired of doing life on my own. I am tired of being the boss of myself. I want to take that first step and I know that it will be painful, but it can't be more painful than what I have already been through…

> In God I trust and am not afraid.
> What can man do to me?
> Psalms 56:11

I thought, what do I have to lose? My life was in shambles, I didn't have any friends and I didn't feel like anybody loved me. So why not take that first step?

What will it cost me? Pain? I've already been in pain. Sorrow? My heart aches with sorrow. Loss of friends? What friends? Family? I have deserted them, and they have given up on me.

So, what will it hurt if I take that first step? And what can man do to me? Let's see, I have been kicked, I have been spat on, I have had fists pounded on my face (many times), cigarettes seared on my legs and the scars from hurtful words penetrate deep into my mind, body and soul. So why wouldn't I take that first step? I'll tell you why.

It's so hard to take that first step because I had gotten so comfortable in my discomfort that I didn't know how to leave that discomfort.

The fear of leaving the only place that was comfortable and familiar, that one place where the pain had numbed my emotions, that place that had paralyzed every part of my being—was now being invaded by the Spirit of God.

God was calling me to take that first step towards Him and He was saying to me, "I have chosen you. I want to save you. I, God your Father, am calling you. Listen to me."

I feared my life would never get better, but I feared God

more. It was not like an "afraid" type of thing. It was more of, "God, change me and love me because I feel no one else wants to."

It was respect, fear and awe; a reverence for God.
But to think that God was choosing me…calling me…
WOW! I had to take that first step, then I read this.

> But you are a chosen people, a royal priesthood,
> a holy nation, God's special possession, that
> you may declare the praises of him who called
> you out of darkness into his wonderful light.
> 1 Peter 2:9

Oh, wow!

After years of knowing the Lord I still get those hair-raising moments! Man, God pulled me out of the darkness and "into His wonderful light!" Amazing! Let's break that down: I am chosen. I am in a royal priesthood dressed in purple. I am holy. I belong to the family of God. God is excellent and He yanked me out of darkness into His marvelous light.

Who wouldn't want that? Come on! Take that first step! You might not understand it all right now, and it may even be fearful, this thing God is asking you to do, but I promise you, He wants to give you a better life and a new family. He wants you to take that first step into the family of God. What do you have to lose? Give Him a chance to show you a better life.

I understand your hesitance. You have been looking for a better life but this God thing…you're not so sure you want to take that step. *What do I have to give up? What do I have to do?* I asked the same questions that you are asking right now. I remember talking to God and saying,

> *"Wait a minute, I like some of my characteristics, there are things about me that I do like! Do I have to change everything? Do I have to give it ALL to you? I gotta think*

about this for a second, this is making me afraid. I got to give up what…and you want what… and I can't say that anymore? Oh, I can't hang with them? Oh, I don't know if I want to do all that! I got to think about all this. God, you are asking a lot of me. Are you asking more than I can give? Please God, can I give you some stuff, some people, some things and I can keep this and that and this? What do you say God, lets compromise you and me?"

Horrifying that I would try to bargain with God (sinful). Why couldn't I trust the Lord with all of me? Why did I try to compromise and keep parts of me to myself? For me, I think it was sin. Sin of arrogance, sin of pride and sin of selfishness. But I came to understand that God loved me so much that He died for me.

> But God demonstrates his own love for us in this:
> While we were still sinners, Christ died for us.
> Romans 5:8

You want to know the truth? I didn't love God enough to give Him all of me because I was selfish. I didn't want to share all of me with Him out of fear, pride and arrogance. But once I understood that God loved me so much that He died on the cross for me, there was nothing I wouldn't give Him. I promise you it takes time. It didn't happen overnight; it was a promise.

But you don't have to wait like I did. You can take that step. Trust me when I say, "The Lord wants to take all of you and bless you, your children and your family."

How can you say *no*?

Take that step and let Him make you a new creation in Christ. Let Him fill your soul with love, happiness and joy.

No one knows more than me how hard it is, and it is a process—I failed numerous times. I would take one step forward and then two steps back. But it's a beautiful thing when you take that step forward and open your heart to the Lord! I promise you will keep going forward for more! God desires nothing more than to give you love, joy, and peace.

> Take delight in the Lord, and he will give you the desires of your heart. 5 Commit your way to the Lord; trust in him and he will do this: 6 He will make your righteous reward shine like the dawn, your vindication like the noonday sun.7 Be still before the Lord and wait patiently for him; do not fret when people succeed in their ways, when they carry out their wicked schemes.
> Psalms 37:4-7

Take that step.

Surrender to Him so that He can begin to reveal Himself to you and He can begin to change your life. He wants to bring you out of darkness and into the light. Trust Him. Don't worry about what others are doing. His focus is You, now make your focus HIM.

TAKE THAT STEP.

Perspective

That word just sounds powerful from the perspective that you need to have a perspective.

What is perspective?

To me, it means you must have good eyes to see through. Where does that begin? Shakespeare said, "Your eyes are the window to your soul." Meaning, you can tell what a person is thinking or who they are based on their perspective.

Where does perspective start? What is the beginning of perspective? How do you see things and what is your perspective on life? How should I act? How should I speak? How should I see things and from whose perspective?

That's the better question: From whose perspective should I determine what life is and how life should be lived?

This could get deep. Hang on and fasten your seat belt.

I never had a perspective on things. I never had a thought or an opinion that mattered much, so I never shared my perspective. I had no worries, as my only perspective was eat, drink and be merry. *What kind of perspective was that,* you say?

Well now, let's get to the real nitty gritty of things. I think the lenses of my eyes were foggy and I could not see clearly. The windows to my soul were darkened by, dare I say it, sin.

There it was: A great black cloud engulfed my soul and took my ability to have perspective and chained me to a life of sin.

Paul talked about this in Romans when he struggled with sin. First, he says:

> So I find this law at work: Although I want to do good, evil is right there with me. 22 For in my inner being I delight in God's law; 23 but I see another law at work in me, waging war against the law of my mind and making me a prisoner of the law of sin at work within me.
> Romans 7:21-23

Here's the big one:

> What a wretched man I am! Who will rescue me from this body that is subject to death? 25 Thanks be to God, who delivers me through Jesus Christ our Lord!
> Romans 7:24-25

WOW!

Decide and stop sitting on the fence.

Who will you serve?

Get some perspective. Is it that you need new eyes? Is it that the fog needs to lift from the window of your heart and your soul needs to find freedom? Paul tells you who will free you from sin—the same God, the same Jesus who freed me. The same Jesus that broke the chains of sin.

What did He give me? HE GAVE ME PERSPECTIVE.

Isn't that what we are looking for...a new perspective? Without Jesus you cannot have perspective. Without Jesus it's impossible to be able to see the vision He has for you. But still you say, *I cannot see what this perspective thing is you are talking about* and *who is this Jesus that can free me from the darkness I live in?*

You know, I spent most of my life looking through a miserable existence of a life filled with sin— like living in bars, in drug-infested houses, selling drugs, hanging with drunks and murderers (yes, murderers), pimps, dealers and thieves. Let me be honest—I would just as soon rob and steal from you, lie to you, manipulate you and then walk away being completely unmoved by your pain. That was my perspective: "Do unto others before they do it to me." I was not even moved by your loss or sorrow. My existence became progressively worse as time went on. I followed the pattern of life that was etched in the membranes of my mind and this is how I became the person I became. Before I knew it, my perspective was darkened by the toxic world I lived in and it became saturated with SIN. Only I did not recognize it as sin because I didn't understand how sinful my life really was.

Maybe you're thinking, *She didn't know it was wrong to do those things?* Well, I did know that some of the things I was doing were wrong, but I didn't understand sin in the context that I was sinning against my Jesus, my God, my Lord. It's different when you don't know the Lord. Things don't seem that bad and you justify, rationalize and minimize your behaviors. But when you give your life to the Lord something happens.

It's kind of like Paul.

Paul was ruthless and one day God blinded him. That was me, I was blinded by my behaviors and actions. In Acts Chapter 9 it talks about Paul still, "Breathing out murderous threats against the Lord's Disciples." I mean this dude was a bad dude. He was just looking for people to take down and more specifically—God's people, whom he hated.

Then as Paul was on his way to Damascus, something happened: God said ENOUGH.

> As he neared Damascus on his journey, suddenly a light from heaven flashed around him.
> 4 He fell to the ground and heard a voice say to him, "Saul, Saul, why do you persecute me?"
> 5 "Who are you, Lord?" Saul asked.
> "I am Jesus, whom you are persecuting," he replied.
> Acts 9:3-5

Jesus confronts Paul, not for attacking his people, but for attacking Him. Paul was directly confronted by the person he was persecuting, and he was about to face the biggest challenge of his life. Would Paul change his perspective? Would Paul's heart be changed? What was he going to do?

What will you do when faced with the challenge to change your perspective? A bigger question is what will you do when challenged to recognize your sin, when Jesus says, "Why are you sinning against the Lord?" because right now, that's the question you are faced with.

It is time to change your perspective and the only way to do that is to do what Paul did. Let's see, what did Paul do... SURRENDER.

> Saul got up from the ground, but when he opened his eyes he could see nothing. So they led him by the hand into Damascus. 9 For three days he was blind, and did not eat or drink anything.
> Acts 9:8-9

Paul was physically blinded for three days, but I think the more important awareness to me was to know that I was spiritually blind for years. Most of my life I was spiritually blind and sinned against Jesus. But you know what? God always has a plan of how He is going to bring us into the Kingdom. It is our job to answer the call when it comes, just as Paul did.

The next step to God's plan was to use a man who feared and did not trust Paul, and probably could not believe that the Lord really wanted him, Ananias, to do what he was being asked to do. God tells this man, Ananias, to go to this house on Straight Street and ask for a man from Tarsus named Paul where, "you will find him praying." It's crazy that the Lord tells Ananias this guy Paul is praying. *Praying?* A few days ago, he was killing people and persecuting Jesus. You can understand the dilemma of Ananias by what he says to the Lord.

> "Lord," Ananias answered, "I have heard many reports about this man and all the harm he has done to your holy people in Jerusalem." 14 And he has come here with authority from the chief priests to arrest all who call on your name."
> Acts 9:13-14

What does Jesus say to Ananias?
A WOW moment, People!

> 15 But the Lord said to Ananias, "Go! This man is my chosen instrument to proclaim my name to the Gentiles and their kings and to the people of Israel. 16 I will show him how much he must suffer for my name."
> Acts 9:15-16

Ananias follows the instructions of the Lord. He finds Paul and places his hands onto Paul's eyes. Paul's eyesight is restored, and Ananias accepts Paul as his brother in Christ. Paul receives the Spirit of God, and so not only were Paul's eyes restored, but Paul was restored spiritually, emotionally, mentally and physically. What did Paul get? PAUL RECEIVED A NEW PERSPECTIVE.

Read the whole story for yourself and see how God restored Paul.

WOW.

The Lord forgave Paul for all of his sinful acts against Him—just as the Lord forgives us. He wants to restore you. God used this man who did dreadful things against Him. If you are thinking, *the things I have done are unforgivable,* you are wrong. I just showed you two people who sinned against the Lord. I did dreadful things in my life. I sinned against my God and yet, He forgave me. He took my life, changed it and is now using it to serve Him by ministering to and teaching others about His love and forgiveness of sins and RESTORATION.

Listen, I know what it feels like to see people doubt you.

I know what it feels like to have people look at you and say, "Naw… you haven't changed, nothing could ever change you." I know what it's like to have people say, "I never thought you would stop doing or saying or acting like that." And it wears on you— the doubters, the haters, those who look at you and do not want to believe you are a new person. What kept me going and helped me stay focused and not give up…? Simple. My perspective and my faith in the Lord and believing what He said to me:

"I WILL NEVER LEAVE YOU NOR FORSAKE YOU. TRUST ME. I LOVE YOU. LET ME GIVE YOU NEW EYES TO SEE AND A NEW HEART."

Thank you, Lord, that you did not give up on me. Thank you, Lord, for a new perspective with new eyes to see. Thank you for your forgiveness as you forgave Paul, who became one of the greatest men to serve You. Amen.

> Therefore, if anyone is in Christ, the new creation has come: The old has gone, the new is here!
> 2 Corinthians 5:17

A NEW PERSPECTIVE.
Amen.

Saturated

What does that mean to be saturated? Good question.

I have found that recently, I have been using that word a lot. I am concerned for the *over* saturation of the mind. I don't think we clearly understand how much damage we do when we over saturate our minds with the things of the world. There was a time in my life that I didn't understand that concept, and I spent years thinking of myself as worthless with feelings of inadequacy, and to be real—not worthy to be loved by anyone.

So, if you haven't read some of my other stuff, you might not know that I am a recovering alcoholic and drug user. I share that because it's not something I hide, and the truth of the matter is that God has delivered me from alcoholism and drug use and any other use I had :) but it was not easy. I spent years battling with the disease and all of the junk left over due to not only my substance use, but also to the consequences of my poor choices—some my fault, and some due to me being a victim of circumstances.

But let's talk specifics.

I was exposed to alcohol at an early age. The first time I drank alcohol for real, I was about thirteen years old. I would steal it out of the fridge and go outside in the dark and drink. By the time I turned seventeen I was living alone in a different city and I was going into bars. I had no problem going into bars and being served. I know I did not look old enough to be in bars, let alone be served alcohol, but I was. Thus, began the saturation process.

Little by little, unknowingly, I was being saturated with the ugliness of the world. I was young and ignorant, and I didn't have the spiritual guidance to know the difference. I could tell you more about myself, but for the sake of this essay, I will limit the information I give you. Plus, if you want to know more about me and the miracles God has done in my life, you will have to read some of my other stuff. :) God is so good.

What I did not know was that the enemy was doing exactly what he set out to do: he used the weaknesses of my mind to make the world look good and convince me that the world could provide for me everything that MY HEART, SOUL, AND MIND CRAVED. This is NOT what the Lord wanted for me.

As I think about that word saturate, and how my life was saturated with all the wrong things which almost destroyed me, I praise God that He saved me from the grips of the enemy. Let's take a look at a verse where the Lord makes very clear what the enemy, Satan, comes to do.

> The thief comes only to steal and kill and destroy. I came that they may have life, and have it to the full.
> John 10:10

WOW.

First, God warns us about what the enemy, Satan, comes to do. If you continue on the path you are on and continue to saturate yourself with the world and all that it has "to offer," it will only destroy your life. Nothing good can come from it as Satan's purpose is to "steal, kill and destroy" and leave you with nothing. Do not spend twenty years of your life wasting away and trusting the world; trusting in the wrong thing.

What you are looking for, God has for you.
He has the answers.

Look, most of my early years I spent being saturated by people, places and things that I thought would bring me love, peace and joy. Here is the image the Lord gave to me a few years back to show me how this saturation process happens: Think of a white T-shirt that is being dyed black, only the shirt is not put in the dye all at once. Imagine it being held up and slowly dipped in and gradually exposed to the dye.

Gradually and slowly, I became darkened by the world until I was SATURATED and looked like the world, or at least the world I was living in. What world was that? Well, my world consisted of drugs and alcohol, lying, cheating, stealing, bad relationships and then more bad relationships. The world I was living in only fed my insecurities and low self-esteem. The world I was living in was saturated with the darkness that can only destroy the mind, body and soul; and, it almost did.

But the Lord had other plans for me.

It took me a minute, ok—a long time, to see that glimmer of hope, but I remember that day. I was sitting in my apartment and looking at the blackened window and I couldn't see any life or light. I was looking for the sun, but it dawned on me that what I was really looking for was a ray of hope.

You know, there's another image the Lord had given to me as a kid and it did not have any significance back then until years later when I looked at that window. I was about fourteen and my teacher had us take a piece of paper and our pencils and we just made like a figure eight all throughout the paper. Then she had us color the circles with different colors. (I had no clue I would remember that silly little picture until years later.) After we colored all the circles in, we covered it with black crayon. Then she had us take a sharp object and just start drawing on it. I noticed the first thing I saw on this black covered paper were these beautiful colors coming through. Years later, when I was looking at that window, I thought of that picture and there on the window was a small glimmer of light. That's what the rest of John 10:10 means, "I came that they may have life and have it abundantly." That glimmer of light was the answer I had been looking for.

I was tired. My mind, body and soul had been saturated by the world and it brought me to my knees. The fear that my children and their children would have this impending darkness on them was greater than staying in the world and it was time to break the generational curse that had plagued the family for, well—generations. The final step was trusting the Lord. I had trusted the world and now, in all my fear, self-doubt and with all of my insecurities and no trust in anything or anyone—I was looking for that one thing that would turn my life around, and not just for me, but for my kids. This was the beginning for me.

Here is what the Lord said to me:

> This day I call the heavens and the earth as witnesses against you that I have set before you life and death, blessings and curses. Now choose life, so that you and your children may live 20 and that you may love the Lord your God, listen to his voice, and hold fast to him. For the Lord is your life, and he will give you many years in the land he swore to give to your fathers, Abraham, Isaac and Jacob.
> Deuteronomy 30:19-20

WOW.

I've got to be honest with you, I didn't fully understand these verses, but I know that God spoke to me that day. I know as I cried out to Him and I remember saying, I don't know who you are, Jesus, but I know that I am tired of being a slave to the world; and like Paul, I said, *Who will save me from this evilness that has saturated and taken over my life?*

As I lay there on the floor an image came over me:

I am in a pool of water being saturated by the world and I'm drowning. I close my eyes as I am going deeper into the depths of despair. I am trying to scream for another breath. I reach my hand up out of the water and through the fogginess I can see a hand reaching towards me. I grab the hand and say, "Yes, I want to be saved! I want life! SATURATE ME WITH YOU, JESUS! BEGIN TO CHANGE ME AND HELP ME TO TRUST YOU. SHOW ME THE WAY!"

The Lord is here for you. Let Him show you the way.

> But seek first his kingdom and his righteousness,
> and all these things will be given to you as well.
> Matthew 6:33

Your first job is to be obedient to the Lord. God is calling you because He wants to change your life. Maybe God has been calling you for a long time? Only you know. Take His hand. He is waiting.

Take the opportunity.

> "Come to me, all you who are weary and
> burdened, and I will give you rest."
> Matthew 11:28

Struggles

I can see the look in your eyes and hear the struggle in your voice when you are trying to convince me that you are on the right path.

You fight to speak and appear confident in what you are saying, it's the external trying to match the internal. I have seen that look before. That face looking back at me saying,

"Are you sure you want to do this alone?"

To which I say,

"Yes, I am sure! I mean, no, I am not sure! What do you mean, do I want to do this alone? Of course not!"

Who wants to be alone?

Who is secure enough to walk this new lifestyle alone? I know the struggle. I hear your thoughts of being alone, depressed and bored. What do I do with these feelings? Who will help me in the dark nights when I'm alone and looking for someone to cling to, talk to and help me get through this? I know you and your struggle fighting these thoughts: the preoccupation with the loss of a loved one, friends who do not want to associate with you because of your new lifestyle—now that you're changing your life, getting clean and stopped drinking. Yeah, I know you.

The struggle of being alone:

"What do you mean you don't want to stay home with me? I thought we were going to watch a movie. I bought popcorn from the theater and ordered pizza."

"Not tonight, sorry, Mom. I just want to be with my friends. Is that ok? Do you mind, Mom?"

"It's ok, Son. Go be with your friends." I will make it through the night, I think.

Although I don't say it, I am thinking— *It's so lonely and I'm so afraid that I will struggle with my thoughts! Who will help me through? Nobody answers my phone calls, and nobody is calling me back. Oh! Let me look at the phone... maybe I missed a call? There are no messages today. Oh, what a struggle this loneliness is! Oh, what a struggle!*

What shall you do?

What did I do? I struggled for so long it took me almost two years to finally say *yes* after twenty plus years of struggling.

> *I want to surrender...? I know the struggle will be hard, but I have to do this! I have to surrender! Yes, fear be gone! The fear of being alone (and I don't even like people!) and the fear of darkness; Oh, the aloneness!*

Now here's a question: HAVE YOU HAD ENOUGH?

Is it worth the pain, the suffering... and not just to you, but to your children and to their children? What do you think— have you had enough? Are you done suffering? Are you done putting your family through the anguish, the nightmares and thoughts of: *Are they drinking? What are they doing? Are they sober? Are they alive? When will the knock on the door come?*

Knock, knock, knock.

> **"We are sorry to inform you, but your daughter was killed in an accident. Please inform her children. Please inform her siblings and family. We're sorry, Ma'am. Please tell her father and anyone else that needs to know. Yes, Ma'am, we do believe it was alcohol or drug related. There were bottles on the floor of the front seat. Yes, Ma'am, we can see you are STRUGGLING to talk**

through your pain. Sorry for your struggle, Ma'am. Yes, Ma'am, we will make sure you get her belongings. Oh, Ma'am, we wanted you to have this, we found it next to her…this picture. A picture of her and this child—we believe it's her son? We're sorry for your struggle and your loss, Ma'am."

Praise God that this is not me or you! If you're reading this, then you have a chance to change things! But it cannot be done on your own.

Paul talks about his struggle in Romans 7. He is specifically referring to sin and his desire to do what is right but continues to do what is wrong. Paul, a man of God, who at one time was NOT a man of God, now recognizes his struggle to do what is right. Listen as Paul describes his struggle and knows that in the end there is only One who can save him from himself, just like there is only One who can save you and me. Listen.

> I do not understand what I do. For what I want to do I do not do, but what I hate I do. 16 And if I do what I do not want to do, I agree that the law is good. 17 As it is, it is no longer I myself who do it, but it is sin living in me. 18 For I know that good itself does not dwell in me, that is, in my sinful nature. For I have the desire to do what is good, but I cannot carry it out. 19 For I do not do the good I want to do, but the evil I do not want to do—this I keep on doing. 20 Now if I do what I do not want to do, it is no longer I who do it, but it is sin living in me that does it.
> 21 So I find this law at work: Although I want to do good, evil is right there with me. 22 For in my inner being I delight in God's law, 23 but I see another law at work in me, waging war against the law of my mind and making me a prisoner of the law of sin at work within me. 24 What a wretched man I am! Who will rescue me from this body that is subject to death? 25 Thanks

> be to God, who delivers me through Jesus Christ our
> Lord! So then, I myself in my mind am a slave to God's
> law, but in my sinful nature a slave to the law of sin.
> Romans 7:15-25

Therein lies the struggle: We want to do the right thing. We want to behave as we should—but we do not.

For years I was STRUGGLING with wanting to do good, be good and look good in the eyes of others but never recognizing that the only one I needed to please was Jesus, my Lord and Savior. The struggle was not my alcoholism, addictions or behaviors—my struggle was my defiance against the Lord to surrender my life to Him so that He could change my life and behaviors and deliver me from sin.

It is true as true can be, I did battle with alcohol and drugs. It is true that my life was disastrous, but the greatest battle and struggle that I fought was my inner-self in the darkness of my soul and mind. There, in the playground of my mind, I kept the truth and all the dark secrets hidden. In the playground of my mind, where no one could see or know the truth of my heart, was the evilness that kept me chained to sin. I must admit that when faced with the external, uncomfortableness of those around me, I would go and hide in the safety of my mind and I never understood or recognized that I was sinking deeper into the abyss. I, like Paul, wanted to do good but continued to do bad. BUT, unlike Paul, I did not recognize that the One who could save me was the One I was running away from. Years of being prayed for, God calling me, being faced with the challenge to surrender and many times even hearing the word of God and still—all I did was IGNORE His call.

> 7 So, as the Holy Spirit says:
> "Today, if you hear his voice, 8 do not harden your
> hearts as you did in the rebellion, during the time of

> testing in the wilderness, 9 where your ancestors tested and tried me, though for forty years they saw what I did. 10 That is why I was angry with that generation; I said, 'Their hearts are always going astray, and they have not known my ways.' 11 So I declared on oath in my anger, 'They shall never enter my rest.'"
> Hebrews 3:7-11

WOW.

When I read those verses, it grasped me like Jesus was reaching down through my mouth and grabbing my very soul. That is exactly what I had been doing all my life—I was hardening my heart and being rebellious—and the struggle now became clear to me.

My struggle was not the sinful acts I was committing, although yes, they were sinful, the struggle was my defiance and rebelliousness against God. The very thing I was looking for, the peace and REST that I was looking for, was right in front of me. I was blinded by the intoxication, the deceitfulness of my drugs, my behaviors and the allure and deception of the enemy. Paul says, "Who will save me from myself? Who will give me sight? Who will save me?"

The same God that gave Paul sight is the exact same God today.

> Jesus Christ is the same yesterday and today and forever.
> Hebrews 13:8

This very minute, if you call on Him, He will give you freedom from yourself and forgive your sins. He will change your life and will break that generational curse put on you as He did for me. He will save you and your children.

> This day I call the heavens and the earth as witnesses against you that I have set before you life and death, blessings and curses. Now choose life, so that you and your children may live.
> Deuteronomy 30:19

> The Lord gives sight to the blind, the Lord lifts those who are bowed down, the Lord loves the righteous.
> Psalm 146:8

> If my people, who are called by my name, will humble themselves and pray and seek my face and turn from their wicked ways, then I will hear from heaven and I will forgive their sin and will heal their land.
> 2 Chronicles 7:14

Are you ready?

Are you ready to stop running your own life and depending on deceitful, blinding eyes that continue to lead you down a destructive path? The Lord saved me. He continued to give me chance after chance. This is your chance.

What does the Lord tell you to do?

Humble yourself. Pray and seek His face, turning from your wicked ways. If you do all these things, then God will what…? THEN, He will hear your cry and most of all— He will forgive you and begin to heal your wounded heart.

Are these words for you? Is this speaking to you? Is this you?

Yes, they are for you. This is YOUR call. Do not wait for the next call because it may be THE call and that will break the Lord's heart and the hearts of those who love you.

Stay in the Boat

I was having a conversation with a friend the other day, and we were talking about these difficult times that we are in and it reminded me about the many storms of my own life.

Several years ago, when I first started in my profession, there was a situation. The agency I had been working at was ending and everyone was panicked, scared and worried.

"What will happen to us? Where are we going to go?" Everyone said and wondered. It was a human response, we all had it and we were all worried.

I remember saying to my coworkers, "God is going to take care of us. God will provide for us. You just have to stay in the boat."

I continued to say that and other reassuring words to them like, *Jesus loves us, and He is going to take care of us.* I believed in what He told me about having faith as small as a mustard seed.

> He replied, "If you have faith as small as a mustard seed, you can say to this mulberry tree, 'Be uprooted and planted in the sea,' and it will obey you."
> Luke 17:6

So, my conversation to them was stay in the boat. When the storms of life attack, we have to believe that the Lord is going to get us through, and He will make a way for us. I could see the stress, fear and uncertainty they were feeling, but I believed what

Jesus continued to instill within me. What did I mean by saying, *stay in the boat...?*"

Well, to understand that phrase we have to go to the word of God.

> 23 Then he got into the boat and his disciples followed him. 24 Suddenly a furious storm came up on the lake, so that the waves swept over the boat. But Jesus was sleeping. 25 The disciples went and woke him, saying, "Lord, save us! We're going to drown! 26 He replied, "You of little faith, why are you so afraid?" Then he got up and rebuked the winds and the waves, and it was completely calm. 27 The men were amazed and asked, "What kind of man is this? Even the winds and the waves obey him!"
> Matthew 8:23-27

I was preaching this very thing to my co-workers, "Stay in the boat, because God is going to take care of and provide for you and me." During that entire time, I can remember preaching to them CONFIDENTLY that God was going to look out for us. But let me tell you this: I am not God and I am not Jesus. I would never pretend to be. Still, if I am ever so arrogant in my conversations with others and I become so sanctimonious that I forget who God is—God forgive me, cause it ain't me.

What I was trying to do was to calm them and help them stay focused on the Lord. I did not want them to forget where their hope was coming from. Their fear was so great, and their anxiety was even greater; and I was no different in that respect. But the difference was—and I don't mean it to sound arrogant—there were some who did not know the Lord, and so now they were seeking for someone or something to rescue them.

Listen, God understands that we are human with fears and anxieties, but God has an expectation when the fears and anxieties of life occur. He does not expect us to sit in our fears and anxieties, He does not want us to sit in our pile of p**p because it is warm and comfortable (sorry). So, what was He telling me to do? Well, I cannot know what He wants me to do if I don't look to Him and ask, *Lord, help me through my anxiety and fears. Help me, help them.*

What does God tell us to do with our fears?

> Humble yourselves, therefore, under God's mighty hand, that he may lift you up in due time. 7 Cast all your anxiety on him because he cares for you.
> 1 Peter 5:6-7

In my times of anxiety, (and trust me, I had it, I can admit that to you) I can remember getting on my knees and praying, *Lord save us! Free me from my anxiety and fears. I trust you, Lord, I know you are going to provide for me and my family. Help me, Lord, to stay focused on you, Lord, and I admit my fears to you, oh Lord!*

Here is what the Lord said to me: "STAY IN THE BOAT. This is a storm you are in. Trust me to take care of you."

So, one of my favorite scriptures is the following.

> For the Spirit God gave us does not make us timid, but gives us power, love and self-discipline.
> 2 Timothy 1:7

I've got to be honest with you, when I first started my walk with the Lord, I had a very difficult time switching off my fears and anxieties that I had to constantly pray and ask the Lord to free me from them. There are times I still struggle with them and so I go back to Him and I pray, Lord it is me again, here I am bringing my fears and anxieties to you. Here I was, telling my co-workers, "Stay in the boat, God is going to take care of you. Just stay prayed up because He is going to provide another job for you."

But I was challenged during this time.

As we got closer to the end, we heard another agency was coming along and would pick up some of the employees. The deal was we had to apply for the positions. So began the process of applying for a new job. It was a scary place to be, but at the same time I was trusting in the Lord to provide. I continued to encourage my co-workers by saying, *We're going to be ok*, over and over. I kept telling them things like: *Trust the Lord! Stay in the boat! Pray to the Lord and know that He is going to provide for you!*

"Fear not, go home and have a good night's sleep. Don't worry," I assured them.

Then it happened. My words came back at me like a boomerang and hit me right between the eyes. Then came the test.

The day came when we were to find out who was going to be hired by this new agency. We were told that the director would be coming over to our office and hand out envelopes to those being hired.

I could hear the excitement as he came in and could see the employees coming out of their offices—some were in the hallway and some were just peaking outside of their door. I decided to wait in my office. I sat quietly knowing that the Lord was going to provide, waiting for my envelope that I just knew I was going to get. I watched him go up and down the hall handing out the envelopes and I remember sitting there as he left the building thinking to myself, *Lord, I am still in the boat.* I didn't understand it. I didn't know what happened. All I knew was that I truly trusted the Lord and if He wanted me at this new agency then why didn't I get an envelope?

My boss walked into my office and said, "I am so sorry. I don't know why you didn't get one."

Here it was, a Friday afternoon at five o'clock, and there was no one to call or ask why I didn't get an envelope. I looked at my boss and I think I said something like, "God is going to take care of me."

I left there a little shook up; I cannot tell you that I was not nervous. But I made a decision that evening that I was going to spend the weekend praying and just turn it over to the Lord. I trusted the Lord so I decided to stay in the boat and ride this storm out believing the Lord would take care of me. I had no idea what He was going to do, but I believed I needed to walk by faith.

> For we live by faith, not by sight.
> 2 Corinthians 5:7

I just believed and prayed and waited for God to work. I knew and understood then that I was being tested.

Ok, you told them to stay in the boat, now what are you going to do?

I was being challenged with everything I had been saying to my coworkers. What are you going to do? I prayed all weekend. I stayed in the Word and went to church. Honestly, I just kept telling the Lord, I *trust you, Lord, I know you are going to provide*.

I went back to work and decided to talk with my boss to ask what happened and why I wasn't hired. She informed me that another person had gotten the position I had applied for because she was more qualified due to a license she had. I waited that week to see what God was going to do and I decided to do nothing but pray.

One day my boss came to me and informed me that I needed to apply for a therapist position at the new agency. She said nothing more, other than apply for the position. I felt the Lord's hand was in this situation, so I followed God's lead and decided to apply for the position.

Soon, I was called and informed I had the position. I was curious about how a position that was not there a week ago all of a sudden was there now? Of course, I knew the Lord's hand was in the situation, but I wanted to know how and who did God use to provide that position. My boss, who had a dual position—

supervisor and therapist—informed them she would stay on as a supervisor, but they had to open her therapist position. So once again—the Lord provided. God used this person, who was not a believer, to provide a position for me. God positioned me where He wanted to position me—God would have His way. Once again, God answered my prayers and calmed the storm.

When you stay in the boat and trust the Lord when you have a storm or conflict—God will calm the waters and will provide a way out. His will, will be done when you believe, trust and obey.

> He replied, "You of little faith, why are you so afraid?" Then he got up and rebuked the winds and the waves, and it was completely calm.
> Matthew 8:26

AMEN.
THANK YOU, LORD! YOU CALM OUR FEARS!
WE LOVE YOU, LORD.

The Well

When I think of a well, I think of a dark place.

I look down, deep into the well, and I recall a time of pain and despair. It was so deep that I did not think I would ever be able to climb out. I remember looking up, from inside the well—looking and asking—*is anyone there and can you save me?*

But no one answered.

Nobody came, nobody heard me, and nobody looked down.

The problem was that I was looking at my circumstances and was distracted, because when I looked up, I only saw the world and what it offered, and I neglected to look at Him. He was there the whole time, but I neglected Him. I wasted so much time. I could have been saved sooner.

> "Turn to me and be saved, all you ends of the earth; for I am God, and there is no other.
> Isaiah 45:22

Every now and then I tried to look up, but I continued to live my life in the well of the world. For years I stayed in the well of discontentment, the well of darkness, pain and emptiness. I would look for ways out and occasionally I could see glimpses of hope, but the weight of the darkness was so very heavy, and I didn't have the strength to pull myself out. I kept thinking, *I can do this*, but my thoughts also kept saying one more drink, one more beer, one more joint, one more, one more… there was always one more *something*. One more bad choice; one more bad decision—it never stopped. I was trapped in the pit of hell—I was trapped in the well. Life had shoved me in, and I began to believe there was no way out and that I was doomed for the rest of my life.

But still, I heard this little voice calling, "You can survive this, you can make it. Look up!"

I would sneak a look and there it was—that light, that glimmer of hope! The problem was that I did not really understand who or what that light represented. I did not know it was Jesus, my ray of Hope.

> When Jesus spoke again to the people, he said, "I am the light of the world. Whoever follows me will never walk in darkness, but will have the light of life."
> John 8:12

I continued to stay in the well because I still didn't understand that He was trying to save me. What was keeping me there? Who or what was I listening to? Why was I so afraid to trust Him?

The world can fill you with fear. Life can convince you that you are not worthy and don't deserve to have better. That is a lie from the pit of hell. Fear can be a paralyzing thing. I used to be afraid that if I fell apart, who would put me back together again? I was convinced that only "good people" deserved a good life. I had been told so many times things like: "You will never amount to anything. You will be found dead at the nearest sewer," and, "You got no chance of being anything other than the loser that you are."

The truth is that when you spend your life hearing that you are not worthy to be loved—you start to believe it. The other problem, to be honest with you, is that I continued to seek out people who thought like me, people who were just as lost as I was; people who were in the well of darkness like me. I was blinded by the darkness and by the lies Satan was telling me. The more I believed that I was unworthy and unlovable, the worse my decisions became. Like Paul on the road to Damascus, when the Lord finally confronted his greatest sin—his defiance and hate for the Lord— and then his eyes were opened. He saw that his acts against God's people were really against the Lord.

Hear what the Lord says to Paul.

> As he neared Damascus on his journey, suddenly a light from heaven flashed around him.
> 4 He fell to the ground and heard a voice say to him, "Saul, Saul, why do you persecute me?"
> 5 "Who are you, Lord?" Saul asked.
> "I am Jesus, whom you are persecuting," he replied.
> Acts 9:3-5

A WOW moment!

It kind of sounds like Paul knew that what he was doing was wrong and who he was wronging.

You ask, *"Didn't you know what you were doing was wrong?"*

Well, the truth of the matter is that before I knew Christ, I picked and chose what I thought was right and wrong. But I was blinded by my foolishness and I was blinded by the world; we become deceived by the world. We lose sight of what is right and wrong until we are brought to our knees, until the well we are in is so deep and the depression, pain and fear becomes so overwhelming, then—we start looking for a way out. It's easy to get lost in the well of deception and it is easy to be manipulated and led astray by our actions especially when we are living in the world. I did not see the real person I was hurting, that the person I was being defiant against was my Lord and Savior. He is who I was hurting, and I did not recognize it because I was not saved; I had not surrendered my life to Him. I had surrendered my life to the world—so I belonged to the world, and I was living in a cesspool of my own making, by my own choices.

But then I heard God say the following to me:

> As has just been said: "Today, if you hear his voice, do not harden your hearts as you did in the rebellion."
> Hebrews 3:15

In my rebellion, I had fallen so deep into the well—in the muck of my life by my own horrible choices. I'm not talking about the choices that others made in their goal to harm to me, I'm only speaking of mine. Yes, many harmed me and caused me pain beyond belief and that pain led to my use of alcohol and drugs—but I still continued in the path of destruction, even after I heard those words, *Don't harden your hearts as you did in the rebellion.*

Why, for two years after I gave my life to the Lord, did I continue to harden my heart? Because I did not feel worthy to be loved. Because the shame and guilt of my life was too much to bear. Because I still returned to the well time after time and continued to fear and reject the light. Simply put, I was not ready to fully surrender and commit to Christ; I was going to the wrong well. I was searching for hope and for someone to love me and He was there all that time. I was thirsty and the water from the well (the world) I was drinking from never seemed to fill the void because it was the wrong well.

I am that woman at the well.

Listen as Jesus has this conversation with the woman at the well. Listen how He tells her who He is, what He wants to give her and how He reveals her own life to her.

He stops to rest by the well while his disciples go into town, of course He knew she would be there, and He asks her for a drink of water. The woman looks at Jesus as if to say, *You're asking me for water...I am not worthy.* But the truth is, Jesus not only knew, but was being compassionate towards her, because she had been rejected and hated by others.

Listen to the exchange:

> Jesus answered her, "If you knew the gift of God and who it is that asks you for a drink, you would have asked him and he would have given you living water." 11"Sir," the woman said, "You have nothing to draw with and the well is deep. Where can you get this living water? 12 Are you greater than our father Jacob, who gave us the well and drank from it himself, as did also his sons and his livestock?" 13 Jesus answered, "Everyone who drinks this water will be thirsty again, 14 but whoever drinks the water I give them will never thirst. Indeed, the water I give them will become in them a spring of water welling up to eternal life." 15 The woman said to him, "Sir, give me this water so that I won't get thirsty and have to keep coming here to draw water." 16 He told her, "Go, call your husband and come back." 17 "I have no husband," she replied. Jesus said to her, "You are right when you say you have no husband. 18 The fact is, you have had five husbands, and the man you now have is not your husband. What you have just said is quite true." 19 "Sir," the woman said, "I can see that you are a prophet."
> John 4:10-19

Jesus was willing to give her living water so that she could live. The question for me was: Was I willing to say *yes* to the one thing that could give me a new life, new hope and forgive my sins or, would I turn my back on the One who wanted to give me living water? Through the whole conversation I could hear the Lord speaking to me just as He was telling the woman: "You are alone, you have been rejected, you keep looking for hope in all the wrong places. STOP. You don't have to continue living this way." Jesus told her about her life, but He was talking to me, and despite my life He was still willing to save me.

He was willing to say, Look, I know the things you have done in your life, but guess what? I have a new way for you.

I was tired of coming to the same well. I was rejected and abandoned because of my own choices, my own doing, but nonetheless—I was tired of always leaving empty. Did you hear what she said to Jesus? The woman said to him, "Sir give me this water so that I won't get thirsty and have to keep coming here to draw water." And here comes the best part, but it's all good—she thinks he is a prophet— but in fact, He is the son of God, our Lord and Savior.

> Then Jesus declared, "I, the one speaking to you—I am he."
> John 4:26

That same Jesus who revealed himself to the woman…guess what?

He is the same Jesus that is revealing himself to us today.

What does His word say? "Don't harden your heart," and, "But whoever drinks the water I give them will never thirst. Indeed, the water I give them will become in them a spring of water welling up to eternal life."

He is the way out. Surrender your life. Do not be afraid.

I had risked my life for the world. Now I made the decision to reject the world and surrender to HIM.

Take His hand. He wants to pull you up and out of the empty well and give you the living water so that you will never thirst again.

Amen.

Acknowledgments

First, let me give thanks to my **Lord and Savior, Jesus Christ,** for dying on the cross and saving me. Thank you, Lord, for giving me a new life filled with hope, mercy and grace.

I would like to thank my children, **Stephen and BJ**, who love me, have forgiven and supported me, and have given me a thumbs up to share my story. Thank you, Sons, for giving me the freedom to express myself in this new venture of sharing with others how the Lord saved me, and provides hope in a hurting world.

I would like to thank my siblings who have loved me, supported me, prayed for me, and forgave me for any hurt I may have caused them. Thank you, **Brothers and Sisters,** for loving me despite myself. Thank you for the many prayers I know you poured out for me throughout my tumultuous life. Thank you for putting up with me and all the heartaches I may have caused you, thank you for your support as God was tearing down the wreckage of my past and rebuilding my life.

Thank you, sister **Rebecky**, for being my accountability partner and for loving me, even when you had to tell me the painful truth. Thank you, Sister, for loving Jesus more than me, for your constant prayers and believing He would save me. Thank you for seeing in me what I could not see myself, that I am fearfully and wonderfully made." (Psalm 139:14)

This work would not have been made possible without the help of one incredibly special you lady, who the Lord pointed out to me. One sunny day, as I looked at her, the Lord said, "She is the one to help you." Thank you, my beautiful niece, **Stella Soto-Crawford**, who without hesitation said to me, "I would be honored to work with you on this project for the Lord." Without hesitation you said, *I want to serve the Lord*. Thank you for your unwavering commitment to be invested in a project you knew little about and continue to work diligently for the Lord. May the Lord bless you.

I want to thank those friends who supported, prayed and gave of their time to read some of the material. Thank you friend, **Delores Williams**, for always believing in me, praying for me and giving up your time to read my material because you love the Lord. You truly are my Sister-in-Christ. Thank you to my **Texting Sisters,** (you know who you are). Your prayers, scriptures and words of encouragement every morning, seven days a week, has poured so much love into my heart. Thank you, Lord, for giving me genuine and loyal friends.

Lastly, I would like to thank **MY MOTHER,** who always encouraged me throughout our times together on Thursday evenings with her boldness and support. I will miss our quiet times, and I will miss our times filled with stories and instructions, "We have to support people, we have to encourage them." You were a social worker long before I became one. Thank you for telling me you were proud of me and proud of all your children. I remember you saying, "My kids are good kids. I am blessed." Thanks, Mom, for our conversations and for the quiet evenings as you watched me work on my computer and I watched you crocheting a masterpiece that only you could make from a simple picture. Thanks, Mom, for that little piece of paper you put in my hand on January 26, 2003, as you watched me struggle. **"We may question ourselves: Do I find favor in the eyes of the Lord? Remembering our weaknesses and failures we realize we have no merit by which God can accept us. But God knows all about us and has provided a way by which we can be accepted by Him. We find grace in God's sight through our relationship with Jesus Christ.**

I know you would have been proud.

Thanks, Mom, I love you and miss you so much.

O. Soto

About the Author

Olga Soto, LSW, LICDC, has worked as a Substance Abuse Therapist for over twenty-five years. She earned an associates in Corrections from the University of Toledo, a BA in Social Work from Lourdes University and then went on to achieve her master's in Rehabilitation Counseling from Bowling Green State University.

Still, her greatest achievement is when she surrendered her life to her Lord and Savior, Jesus Christ, which was the beginning of her transformation.

Her life's purpose can be understood through the example of Joseph, found in the first book of the bible, Genesis.

"You intended to harm me, but God intended it for good to accomplish what is now being done, the saving of many lives." (Genesis 50:20)

"God has been preparing me for this very day." – Olga Soto

Olga Soto lives in Toledo, Ohio, right around the corner from her beloved mother, Hortense.

Be Encouraged, Volume 2
The Lie

By Olga Soto

Let's look at the meaning of a lie which can at times, in our minds, look like a truth when it comes from the pit of hell.

John 10:10 tell us, "The thief comes only to steal and kill and destroy; I have come that they may have life, and have it to the full."

The TRUTH is that the enemy has been stealing God's children for a lifetime—my lifetime and yours. We have all had thoughts in our minds about ourselves, thoughts that were planted by the enemy since the beginning of our time.

What is a lie?

The definition of a lie is: an assertion of something known or believed by the speaker or writer to be untrue with intent to deceive; something that misleads or deceives.

Did you hear that?

What is the purpose of this deception? To separate us from the person making the statement? To separate us from those who are supposed to love us? To separate us from the TRUTH.

Yes, that's it. To separate us from God, from the one who is trying to save us and show us the TRUTH.

Here is what God's word tells us:

> Then you will know the truth, and
> the truth will set you free.
> John 8:32

I didn't know the TRUTH. I always believed the lies.
You are worthless. You will never amount to anything.

You are stupid.
I was held hostage by the beliefs in my own head.

> *Oh Lord, thank you for freeing me from the negativity in my mind, from the lie! Thank you, Lord, that I finally surrendered, and thank you, God, for giving me the courage to trust you and begin to let go of the lie. Oh Lord, thank you for showing me the truth. Your TRUTH.*

The enemy has one goal, which is to keep us hostage from the TRUTH and to keep us believing we will never amount to anything. As the days go by, the lie gains such strength, like a storm that begins with a gust of wind, gradually gaining strength by every word that is filtered into our thoughts. As years pass, our minds are held captive by these lies and we become weak and unable to get free from its chains.

I believed those lies and felt there was no way out, that there was nothing or anyone that would free me from the lie.

> *I must be worthless. I must be dumb, it's true. This must be my destiny, to be a nobody and never amount to anything. I might as well turn to something that will help me feel better about myself. Oh, look! Alcohol! You make me feel so good, you think I am beautiful you will save me from myself, you will free me from this feeling of worthlessness. Wait, you are temporary? I don't feel good, things are getting worse. What? I gave my life to you; I believed you for years! I don't want to die! I have trusted in the lie and exchanged it for another lie...*

Discover how The Lie ends in

Be Encouraged, Volume 2
Coming soon in 2023!!

Made in the USA
Monee, IL
04 February 2023